I0820295

YOU ARE
MY
ANSWERED
PRAYER

♥

YOU ARE MY ANSWERED PRAYER

A Keepsake of the LOVE STORY God Gave Us

Jen Thompson

The authorised representative in the EEA is Simon and Schuster Netherlands BV, Herculesplein 96 3584 AA Utrecht, Netherlands. (info@simonandschuster.nl)

AMEN Editions
an imprint of Andrews McMeel Publishing
a division of Andrews McMeel Universal
1130 Walnut Street, Kansas City, Missouri 64106

www.ameneditions.com

26 27 28 29 30 RLP 10 9 8 7 6 5 4 3 2 1

ISBN: 978-1-5248-9992-9

Library of Congress Control Number: 2025943273

Editor: Jennifer Leight
Design: Melissa Gerber
Production Manager: Tamara Haus

Illustrations used under license from Shutterstock

This love story celebrates
the sacred bond between
two beloved children of God:

____

&

____

I CAN SEE THE TENDER BRUSHSTROKES of God covering every moment of my life as I look back over the years. His love, grace, mercy, kindness, faithfulness, provision, and healing have seeped into every second I've been gifted. All the spaces and cracks are filled. Even the parts that seem broken and torn have been carefully mended by His hand.

I remember every prayer uttered in the night. Every plea lifted up to heaven. Every cry of gratitude, every word of longing. I see how each one has been held in His loving arms.

And in a whisper, the wind carries His promises back to me:

I am seen.
I am loved.
I am known.
I am covered in grace.

He hears my prayers.

They may not always be answered in the ways I had hoped or imagined, but I trust they are always answered in the ways that are best. Our God is good, and He sees the full picture—far beyond what we can understand.

One of the greatest answers to my prayers has been the gift of my relationship with my husband—my love, my best friend, my closest companion. We've walked through valleys, soared near mountaintops, and traveled many winding roads in between. Through it all, I've seen God's hand at work, covering this masterpiece we call our love with care, intention, and grace.

I am praying the same for every couple who opens these pages.

As you move through each prompt, I pray your relationship with God and one another grows deeper than you imagined. I pray you feel His provision, learn new things about each other, and untangle anything that needs to be gently restored. I pray for healing conversations and dreams rekindled. I pray that what happens in these pages seeps into the everyday rhythm of your life together.

I pray you remember the prayers you've spoken in the night and the hopes you've carried in the morning. That you see His fingerprints all over your love story. And that when you look at each other, you recognize it without question:

You are my answered prayer.

Truly Yours, Jen

Look Back, Look Up, Look Forward

In these pages, you'll find a space to reflect, celebrate, and deepen your relationship—with both God and each other. Every entry is an invitation to honor your love and faith. You'll find:

- A Scripture verse to center your hearts
- A short reflection to stir gratitude for your life together
- A thoughtful prompt to cherish your story so far or dream boldly about what's still to come
- A closing prayer to lift your love up to God

There's no single path to follow. Feel free to move in order or skip to what calls to you. However you journey through, let this be a sacred place where your hearts meet. And remember: What you build here in this time together is part of your love story too.

Every good and perfect gift is from above.

—JAMES 1:17A (NIV)

When we first met, how could we have known that God had blessed us with a gift we would get to unwrap each and every day? It's amazing to think about all that we bring into our life together—simply by being who God created each of us to be.

Just a few of the gifts God has given me through you:

1 ______________________________

2 ______________________________

3 ______________________________

Your turn:

1 ______________________________

2 ______________________________

3 ______________________________

God of All Seasons, Guide us to continue to discover new blessings in each other and in our love, just as You designed it. That's one of the greatest gifts of being in a relationship that lasts a lifetime. What a treasure it is to grow through every stage by each other's side. Amen.

“SEE, I AM DOING A NEW THING! NOW IT SPRINGS UP; DO YOU NOT PERCEIVE IT?”

—ISAIAH 43:19A (NIV)

Our God is all about new beginnings—even the kind we can’t recognize. Whether it was sweet, awkward, or magical, our first date marked the start of something beautiful. We can now smile knowingly at the nerves, the curiosity, that spark of something we couldn’t quite name yet. Sure enough, God was already at work in our story.

This is what I remember most about our first date:

____

____

____

Your turn:

____

____

____

God of New Beginnings, Thank You for that
first step—the moment our journey began.
Help us to keep that sense of wonder alive,
to always delight in one another, and to see
Your hand in every chapter of our story. Amen.

Many are the plans in a person's heart, but it is the LORD's purpose that prevails.

—PROVERBS 19:21 (NIV)

Looking back now, it all makes perfect sense. It makes *God* sense. When we think about where we would be without God guiding us to each other . . . well, let's not even go there. Our hearts would be left wanting.

This is when I knew God had placed you on His desired path for me:

Your turn:

Lord of Perfect Purpose, What a gift it is to walk hand in hand, in love so deeply. Thank You for going before us and making a way for us to be together. In Your wisdom, Your purpose for us was each other. May we continue to walk Your paths with Your love and our love to light the way. Amen.

TWO ARE BETTER THAN ONE.

—ECCLESIASTES 4:9A (NIV)

Our friends and family may say we're opposites in many ways. But in God's grand plan, He brought us together to complement one another—our strengths filling in where the other may be blind. In the most tender ways, our differences create balance, revealing how beautifully we were made to walk this journey side by side.

Together, we are . . .

Creator God, We praise You for making us to fit together so nicely. Help us to each continue bringing our unique gifts to our together table. Our lives are so much better because of Your wisdom in filling our love with Your ways. Amen.

"Truly, I tell you, if you say to this mountain, 'Be taken up and thrown into the sea,' and if you do not doubt in your heart but believe that what you say will come to pass, it will be done for you."

—MARK 11:23 (NRSVUE)

We are foolish if we believe that any relationship can move forward without hitting at least occasional obstacles. But You don't leave us in the struggle if we turn to You. Your love is always ready to lift up our love.

Our faith in God has already helped us move these mountains in our relationship:

____

____

____

These are the mountains we are still praying in confidence for Him to move:

____

____

____

Waymaker, Thank You for the mountains You have moved and those You will continue to move for us. We see Your miracles each day and trust in Your goodness. You go before us, making a way when none seems possible. In both small and mighty ways, You are always at work in our lives. Amen.

YOUR LOVE, GOD, IS MY SONG, AND I'LL SING IT!

—PSALM 89:1A (MSG)

Every great love story has a soundtrack. We lift our voices in worship as tears stream down our cheeks in a moment of deep connection with our God above. We sway in each other's arms on our wedding day, lost in the song we call ours. Music has a way of moving our hearts.

The playlist of our love blessed by God:

Conductor of Our Lives, Thank You for weaving music into our hearts and filling our love story with songs of joy, grace, and devotion. Keep our hearts in harmony with each other and with You, singing Your love (the best song of all!) through every season. Amen.

Let all that you do be done in love.

—1 CORINTHIANS 16:14 (NRSVUE)

Father, let all we do be done in love. Holy Spirit, let all we do be done in love. Jesus, let all we do be done in love. What if we made this the beautiful prayer of our marriage? In moments of selfishness or frustration, may the Holy Spirit give us a gentle nudge. And may Jesus show us how to love as He loved.

One of the ways you show me love is when you . . .

____

____

____

Your turn:

____

____

____

Love Himself, You are the source of perfect love. When we fix our eyes on You and surrender our thoughts, our words, and our actions to Your guidance, love flows more freely through us and between us. Strengthen the bond we share and let our love reflect the fullness of Yours. Amen.

LET THE FAVOR OF THE LORD OUR GOD BE UPON US. AND MAKE THE WORK OF OUR HANDS STAND STRONG.

—PSALM 90:17A (NLV)

The ordinary rhythms of our life together seem somehow sacred. The morning coffee routine, cleaning up after dinner, the way we check in before bed. These simple habits may seem small, but they're part of what makes our relationship feel steady and safe. Our routines are reminders that we choose each other—day in and day out.

One small routine or daily habit we've built that brings me comfort or joy:

____

____

____

Your turn:

____

____

____

God of Ordinary Days, Thank You for the gift of daily life together. Help us see the beauty in the routines we share and fill them with intention, gratitude, and love. May our small habits be acts of devotion—to You and to each other. Amen.

From his fullness we have all received, grace upon grace.

—JOHN 1:16 (NRSVUE)

We all need grace. I need it. You need it. Our relationship needs it. Thankfully, through Jesus, we've received it in abundance—grace upon grace upon grace. We will fall short. We will hurt each other sometimes. But we aren't defined by our shortcomings. We are invited to confess, forgive, and move forward, held together by the love of Jesus that covers it all.

Thank you for all the times you've shown me grace. One moment I'll never forget is when . . .

____

____

____

Your turn:

____

____

____

♥

Giver of Grace, Thank You for meeting us with mercy again and again. May we be quick to turn our wrongs over to You, apologize to one another, and move forward even stronger in our relationship with one another and with You—blanketed in Your grace and Your love. Amen.

BUT THEY WHO WAIT UPON THE LORD WILL GET NEW STRENGTH. THEY WILL RISE UP WITH WINGS LIKE EAGLES. THEY WILL RUN AND NOT GET TIRED. THEY WILL WALK AND NOT BECOME WEAK.

—ISAIAH 40:31 (NLV)

Seasons of waiting aren't easy, but we're never left to wait alone. We can lean into the Lord and on each other. We can pray, encourage, and remind one another that God's strength is our hope. Even when it feels like a marathon, His promise remains. We will run and not grow weary, walk and not grow weak.

When we're in waiting places, you encourage me by . . .

____

____

____

Your turn:

____

____

____

Strength Renewer, Thank You for being near in the pauses and the in-betweens. Teach us to wait well—with hope, patience, and love in You and for one another. Help us to be a steady source of strength and comfort to each other, trusting that You are always working—even in the waiting. Amen.

For we are God's handiwork, created in Christ Jesus to do good works, which God prepared in advance for us to do.

—EPHESIANS 2:10 (NIV)

There will only ever be one you, one me, one love story like ours. It's tempting to compare ourselves to couples in highlight reels. But the beauty is in the life we're building that's uniquely ours. God didn't create us to copy anyone else. He made us to reflect Him in a way no one else could.

I love these quirky or uncommon things about our relationship:

____

____

____

Your turn:

____

____

____

Creator, Thank You for making us so wonderfully unique—not just as individuals, but as a couple. Help us resist the pull of comparison and instead cherish what You're building in us. May we never lose sight of all that we bring to the table together, just by being who You made us to be. Amen.

THIS IS THE DAY THAT THE LORD HAS MADE; LET US REJOICE AND BE GLAD IN IT.

—PSALM 118:24 (NRSVUE)

This day. This moment. Right here. Just the two of us, sharing Scripture, talking, and praying. What a gift it is to grow in faith and in love. Every day together is worth celebrating. Not just the big milestones, but the little joys too—quiet (or even crazy) mornings, shared laughter, answered prayers, and the grace we find in the ordinary.

Something I'm rejoicing over right now that I want to share with you:

____

____

____

Your turn:

____

____

____

Lord of All Our Days, Thank You for the beauty of today—for breath in our lungs, love in our hearts, and the joy of walking, eating, sleeping, and rejoicing side by side. Keep us aware of the shared blessings around us and help us celebrate each day together as the gift that it is. Amen.

I found the one my heart loves.

—SONG OF SONGS 3:4A (NIV)

Our love story is a breathtaking gift—uniquely ours, beautifully written by the hand of a faithful God. It's a story we hold close. One we will never tire of telling. One we will never tire of reliving. And it continues to grow through answered prayers and unexpected turns. That might just be the best part. Every chapter matters.

My favorite part of our love story so far is . . .

____

____

____

Your turn:

____

____

____

God of the Universe, Thank You for orchestrating our story with care and intention. For every step that brought us together and every moment still to come, we give You praise. Help us treasure the journey, share the joy, and always keep You at the center of our love. Amen.

AND HE GIVES GRACE GENEROUSLY. AS THE SCRIPTURES SAY, "GOD OPPOSES THE PROUD BUT GIVES GRACE TO THE HUMBLE."

—JAMES 4:6 (NLT)

Sometimes our pride gets the better of us. It keeps us from asking for help—from each other and from God. We carry more than we were meant to, pretending we're fine when we're not. But we weren't made to go it alone. God invites us to come with humble hearts. To ask. To receive. To let grace meet us where we are.

What are we really good at immediately turning over to God?

When are we able to easily accept help from each other?

What do we still try to carry alone (and it shows)?

Father God, You meet us with outstretched arms every time we lay our pride aside. Guide us to ask for help—with honesty, not hesitation. Help us to receive Your grace and one another's love with open hands and humble hearts. Amen.

Beloved, let us love one another, because love is from God; everyone who loves is born of God and knows God.

—1 JOHN 4:7 (NRSVUE)

God loves us, and we love each other. It's the most beautiful exchange—a holy flow of love we're invited into every single day. His love for us. My love for you. Your love for me. It's sacred. Life-giving. Something I'll never take for granted.

There are so many reasons I love you, but today these three come to mind:

____

____

____

Your turn:

____

____

____

Giver of Love, Thank You for pouring Your love into us so freely. Teach us to love each other the way You love—with patience, kindness, and joy. Let our love reflect Your heart, and may we never lose sight of the incredible gift it is to love and be loved. Amen.

THOUGH HE BRINGS GRIEF, HE WILL SHOW COMPASSION, SO GREAT IS HIS UNFAILING LOVE.

—LAMENTATIONS 3:32 (NIV)

We will walk down roads of grief together. Sometimes your heart will break, and I'll be the one to hold you up. Other times, I'll need you to carry me for a while. What a comfort it is to know that even in those painful seasons, love remains. What a gift that we can lean into our love and rest in His love that holds everything together.

When my heart has been broken, one way that you've loved me well is by . . .

Your turn:

Compassionate One, You wrap us in Your unfailing love in times of joy and in times of grief. Help us find healing in Your compassion when our hearts are breaking, and show us how we can love each other well in our times of grief. Amen.

“Until now you have not asked for anything in my name. Ask and you will receive, and your joy will be complete.”

—JOHN 16:24 (NIV)

Jesus invites us to ask wholeheartedly in His name. He promises that when we do, our joy will be complete. But how often do we actually trust in this way? Instead of getting lost in the daily distractions, let’s remember that we have a loving Father who delights in hearing from us and longs to give us the desires of our hearts.

Tell me the desires of your heart, and I will tell you mine. Then let's pray together in His name for these blessings.

God Who Hears Us, May we not forget to lift everything up to You. Guide us to bring You the desires of our hearts and to approach Your throne of joy boldly each and every day. We know that You listen lovingly, and we trust that You will provide. Amen.

HE WHO FINDS A WIFE FINDS A GOOD THING AND OBTAINS FAVOR FROM THE LORD.

—PROVERBS 18:22 (NRSVUE)

You, my love, are a good thing. Let's never lose sight of the goodness we each bring into this relationship. Even in the moments when we're not seeing eye to eye, that doesn't mean we've lost what makes us good together. It just means there's something to work through—and working through it, with love and grace, can draw us even closer.

You are a good thing in my life. Let me tell you why:

____

____

____

Your turn:

____

____

____

Wise Provider, Thank You for the goodness we see in one another and the favor You've shown us in bringing us together. Help us hold on to that goodness and appreciation, even on the hard days. Remind us of the gift we have in each other and lead us through every challenge with love. Amen.

"Peace I leave with you; my peace I give you. I do not give to you as the world gives. Do not let your hearts be troubled and do not be afraid."

—JOHN 14:27 (NIV)

The peace Jesus offers is unlike anything the world can give. When our life feels heavy and circumstances threaten to overwhelm us, we can cling to Him. He meets us right there—in the middle of the chaos—and gently leads us into the safety and comfort of His peaceful embrace.

One time we've felt peace that didn't make sense in the circumstances:

____

____

____

Your turn:

____

____

____

Peacemaker, Thank You for the kind of peace that quiets fear and steadies our hearts. Help us to turn to You when the world feels loud and uncertain. Remind us that Your peace is always available—freely given, deeply lasting, and never out of reach. Amen.

AND WE KNOW THAT IN ALL THINGS GOD WORKS FOR THE GOOD OF THOSE WHO LOVE HIM, WHO HAVE BEEN CALLED ACCORDING TO HIS PURPOSE.

—ROMANS 8:28 (NIV)

There will be times when life simply doesn't feel good. But even then, ***God*** is still good. Trusting Him doesn't mean pretending everything is fine. It means believing His purpose is unfolding, even when we can't see it yet. In every struggle, we can cling to the truth that His goodness never fails and His plans are always at work.

Verses we can turn to that will always remind us of God's goodness:

Our Good God, Even when our circumstances feel uncertain, You remain steady. Help us to hold fast to Your promises and to trust that You are always working—behind the scenes, within our hearts, and for our good. In You we forever find love and purpose. Amen.

Be on your guard; stand firm in the faith; be courageous; be strong.

—1 CORINTHIANS 16:13 (NIV)

Standing firm, courageous, and strong can sometimes feel difficult. But the good news is, we don't stand alone. We stand together, arms linked, hearts lifted, with our eyes fixed on our Father above. We stand firm not in our own power, but in our faith. In God's promises. In His love that never fails.

A small, everyday act of courage I've seen in you is . . .

____

____

____

Your turn:

____

____

____

Giver of Courage and Strength, We give thanks that there is nothing we face alone. Not only do we have each other, but we have You, anchoring us when the winds of life threaten to knock us down. We will not fall. We will stand firm—in You. Amen.

“HE CALLS HIS OWN SHEEP BY NAME AND LEADS THEM OUT.”

—JOHN 10:3B (NIV)

There’s a special kind of love in the names we call each other. Whether sweet, silly, or sacred, nicknames are a language of affection—spoken with smiles, whispered in quiet, texted in the middle of busy days. They remind us we’re seen, cherished, and known in a way no one else understands. They reflect the bond we’ve built and the joy we share.

These are some of the nicknames we use for each other—and what they mean to me:

____

____

____

Your turn:

____

____

____

Loving Father, Thank You for the joy of intimacy and the comfort of closeness. Help us continue to speak to one another with kindness and delight—even in the little things like nicknames. May our words always reflect the deep love and honor we have for one another, rooted in Your love for us. Amen.

Be devoted to one another in love. Honor one another above yourselves.

—ROMANS 12:10 (NIV)

Love isn't always loud. (Remember that even God was in a whisper—not the earthquake or fire—with Isaiah in 1 Kings 19.) Sometimes love looks like a cup of coffee brought to bed. A kind word in a tense moment. A hand held in silence. These quiet offerings are sacred too—small acts that say "You matter" without any words.

Here are some of the quiet ways you've made me feel deeply loved:

Your turn:

God of Gentle Strength, Help us never to overlook the little things. Remind us that even silent service sings when it's offered in love. May our days be filled with kindness, mutual honor, and the joy of simply being there for one another. Amen.

THE GENEROUS WILL PROSPER; THOSE WHO REFRESH OTHERS WILL THEMSELVES BE REFRESHED.

—PROVERBS 11:25 (NLT)

Some gifts are wrapped in paper and ribbon. Others are wrapped in time, thoughtfulness, or sacrifice. From handwritten notes to surprise getaways, from simple tokens to cherished collectibles, we've given each other more than things. We've given pieces of our hearts.

A gift you've given me that still makes me smile:

____

____

____

Your turn:

____

____

____

♥

Generous God, Thank You for the gift of each other and the many ways we've expressed love through giving. Teach us to be generous with more than gifts—generous with grace, with patience, with attention. May every gift we share be a reflection of Your endless love. Amen.

But the fruit of the Spirit is love, joy, peace, patience, kindness, goodness, faith.

—GALATIANS 5:22 (WEB)

The fruit of the Spirit is within us, fully ripe and ready to nourish our lives and our love. As we turn our gaze from the things of this world to His daily gifts, we're reminded of what we get to share: Love. Joy. Peace. Patience. Kindness. Goodness. Faithfulness. Sweet, sustaining fruit—and a blessing to offer one another.

The fruit of the Spirit I see most in you is . . .

Your turn:

Holy Spirit, Thank You for the gifts You bestow on us and grow in us each day. Help us to notice them, nurture them, and generously offer them to one another. May our relationship be rooted in these fruits and honor Your love at work in us. Amen.

A CHEERFUL HEART IS GOOD MEDICINE.

—PROVERBS 17:22A (NLT)

Every couple has those moments—the ones that make us cringe and laugh at the same time. Maybe spinach teeth on date night or forgetting to pack pants on vacation. But oddly, those moments are precious. They remind us that love isn't perfect—it's real. It blushes, giggles, and bonds us through awkwardness. And best of all, it always finds a way to laugh together.

An embarrassing shared moment that we can laugh about now:

____

____

____

Your turn:

____

____

____

God of All Grace, Thank You for the gift of laughter and the bond it creates. Help us not to take ourselves too seriously and to always find joy—even in the most awkward, silly, or embarrassing moments. Let our laughter be part of the glue that keeps us close. Amen.

Love bears all things, believes all things, hopes all things, endures all things. Love never ends.

—1 CORINTHIANS 13:7–8A (RSV)

Some days are full of sunshine and laughter. Others, we walk through storms hand in hand. But *always* our love is still standing. It's not perfect, but it's planted deep in grace. Rooted in faith. Watered by prayer. And through it all, God continues to grow us stronger.

We've weathered these storms together with God's help:

____

____

____

We've learned to dance in the rain by:

____

____

____

Faithful Father, Thank You for being our shelter in every storm. Strengthen our bond when trials come. Teach us to be soft where the world turns hard, and remind us that endurance is part of love's beauty. Let our story sing of Your faithfulness. Amen.

THEY BROKE BREAD IN THEIR HOMES AND ATE TOGETHER WITH GLAD AND SINCERE HEARTS.

—ACTS 2:46B (NIV)

There's something sacred about sharing a meal together—slowing down, making space, and reconnecting. Around the table, we laugh, reflect, nourish, and remember we belong to each other. Whether it's a quiet dinner at home, a picnic in the park, or a celebration with family, meals have a way of bringing us back to what matters most.

One meal I'll never forget sharing with you was . . .

____

____

____

Your turn:

____

____

____

Provider of Every Good Thing, Thank You for the daily bread we receive and the joy of sharing it together. Bless our table, our conversations, and the moments that fill us with more than food. May we never take for granted the beauty of nourishing both body and soul, side by side. Amen.

Let everyone be quick to listen, slow to speak, slow to anger.

—JAMES 1:19B (NRSVUE)

Even in deep love, communication can get tangled with a misread look or a misunderstood tone. But these moments can become opportunities to grow closer. When we choose to listen and learn, we begin to "translate" each other's hearts more clearly. What once felt confusing starts to feel familiar. That's the kind of intimacy that only time and grace can build.

One thing you've learned to "translate" in how I express feelings:

____

____

____

Your turn:

____

____

____

God of Understanding, Thank You for the gift of communication and the grace to grow through misunderstandings. Help us to keep listening with compassion, speaking with care, and learning each other's hearts more fully every day. Amen.

I HAVE MUCH TO WRITE TO YOU, BUT I DO NOT WANT TO USE PAPER AND INK. INSTEAD, I HOPE TO VISIT YOU AND TALK WITH YOU FACE TO FACE, SO THAT OUR JOY MAY BE COMPLETE.

—2 JOHN 1:12 (NIV)

Can you imagine if we had to spend our days apart, only connecting through written words? Even in today's world of texts and emails, we know something special happens when we speak face-to-face. Joy comes in knowing glances, shared laughter, gentle nods of understanding. Let's keep choosing conversation over convenience, togetherness over distraction, and eye contact over screen time.

One face-to-face moment with you I'll always treasure is . . .

Your turn:

Joy Giver, Thank You for the gift of one-on-one time and face-to-face connection. Help us to never take that for granted, to keep looking into each other's eyes. Slow us down, lift our heads, and open our hearts to see one another clearly. May our joy be made full in the time we share. Amen.

Let the peace of Christ rule in your hearts, since as members of one body you were called to peace. And be thankful.

—COLOSSIANS 3:15 (NIV)

There's a sacred kind of peace that fills a home built with love, patience, and prayer. We don't need to walk a perfect path, but we do try to choose calm even when chaos knocks. Together, we've come to understand that true peace is not the absence of noise but the abiding presence of Christ.

These are the ways we protect the peace in our relationship:

____

____

____

Here's what peace looks like in our daily life together:

____

____

____

Prince of Peace, You teach us to seek stillness in a world of busyness. Let Your peace reign in our home, in our hearts, and in every word we speak to one another. Thank You for being the ever-present calm in our messy lives. Amen.

THE HEAVENS PROCLAIM THE GLORY OF GOD. THE SKIES DISPLAY HIS CRAFTSMANSHIP.

—PSALM 19:1 (NLT)

It's amazing how stepping outside together helps us breathe a little deeper and hold each other a little closer. Maybe it's a shared walk at sunset, or the peace of sitting under the stars. God's creation has a way of grounding us and reminding us of what really matters.

An outdoor memory we've shared that I treasure:

____

____

____

Your turn:

____

____

____

Creator of Heaven and Earth, Thank You for the beauty of this world and the gift of sharing it together. Whether it's blue skies or stormy weather, let us never forget the joy of walking side by side beneath Your handiwork. May the world outside our door always draw us closer to each other—and to You. Amen.

But you, O Lord, are a God merciful and gracious, slow to anger and abounding in steadfast love and faithfulness.

—PSALM 86:15 (NRSVUE)

Merciful. Gracious. Patient. Steadfast. Faithful. These aren't just attributes of our amazing God. They're also beautiful guides for how we can love one another well as we walk together through the good days and the bad days and all the in-between.

You showed me [*attribute*] when you [*action*], and it made me feel [*emotion*].

____

____

____

Your turn:

____

____

____

Merciful and Gracious God, Thank You for being our example of love that never gives up and never grows cold. Teach us to be patient when it's hard, faithful when it's inconvenient, and kind even when we're tired. Let our love be shaped by Yours—steadfast, gentle, and full of grace. Amen.

EVERY TIME I THINK OF YOU, I GIVE THANKS TO MY GOD.

—PHILIPPIANS 1:3 (NLT)

Love often lives in the little things. In the rhythm of the day, in the sounds, scents, and scenes that pass without ceremony. A favorite song on the radio. The smell of coffee. A phrase only we say. These ordinary moments become extraordinary because they remind us of each other. They turn an average day into something tender. Familiar. Beautiful.

When I see these things in the middle of any ordinary day, I think of you:

____

____

____

Your turn:

____

____

____

Author of Our Story, Thank You for filling our lives with gentle reminders of love. Help us not to overlook the sacred tucked into the simple. Teach us to treasure the ways You bring us together—again and again—in the quiet beauty of everyday life. Amen.

Jesus wept.

—JOHN 11:35 (NIV)

Two words. But they carry the full weight of love, loss, and compassion. We are never alone in our grief or struggle. Jesus understands it all—and He meets us there. And so do we, for one another. In the hard moments, we don't have to fix everything. Sometimes, the most sacred thing we can do is simply stay, hold space, and let love speak through our tears.

A time I felt deeply seen or comforted by you was . . .

Your turn:

God Who Weeps with Us, Thank You for being so near to the brokenhearted. Teach us how to show up for each other with tenderness, without rushing to solve or explain. Help us carry one another's burdens with gentleness and grace. May our tears be safe with each other, just as they are with You. Amen.

SING FOR JOY O HEAVENS, AND EXULT, O EARTH; BREAK FORTH, O MOUNTAINS, INTO SINGING!

—ISAIAH 49:13A (NRSVUE)

What a beautiful image of creation itself bursting into song! The heavens, the earth, the mountains all lifting their voices in worship. And somehow, when I'm worshipping with you by my side, I feel like we're part of that chorus. In those moments, I sense such a joyful connection not only to the Lord, but also to you and the plans He has for us together.

A time I felt especially connected to you and to the Lord in worship was . . .

Your turn:

Joyful One, Thank You for the gift of shared worship. Whether in a sanctuary, a car, or our living room, draw our hearts closer to You and to each other. Let our praises rise together like the mountains breaking into song—and may joy always be part of the soundtrack of our love. Amen.

So Jacob served seven years to get Rachel, but they seemed like only a few days to him because of his love for her.

—GENESIS 29:20 (NIV)

Time shifts when love is at the center. What once felt long and difficult becomes fleeting when your heart is full. When I think about all we've walked through, I'm amazed at how quickly it's flown. Not because life was always easy, but because loving you makes every season sweeter and every moment more meaningful than I ever imagined.

A season of waiting or working that felt easier simply because I had you was . . .

Your turn:

God of Lasting Promise, Thank You for the kind of love that gives meaning to time—love that endures, that sacrifices, and that sees joy even in the waiting. Help us treasure every day we have together and serve one another with glad and generous hearts. Amen.

LET YOUR CONVERSATION BE ALWAYS FULL OF GRACE, SEASONED WITH SALT.

—COLOSSIANS 4:6A (NIV)

We've built our own little world, and with it, a language all our own. Maybe it's a phrase that no one else would understand or a look that says everything. These inside jokes and shared expressions are more than silly. They are a shared vocabulary for a shared life. A way for us to communicate "I get you."

Some phrases or looks we use that only we understand (and I cherish that):

____

____

____

Your turn:

____

____

____

God of Connection, Thank You for the gift of laughter, shared smiles, and silly words that belong only to us. May our communication always be laced with love and seasoned with playfulness. Amen.

Love the Lord your God with all your heart and with all your soul and with all your strength.

—DEUTERONOMY 6:5 (NIV)

When we love God with that kind of fullness, it overflows into our words, our choices, the way we love each other. We won't always get it right. Some days we're tired or distracted. But God desires wholehearted love—imperfect yet sincere. And when we seek Him together, we stay grounded in what matters most: loving God and loving each other well.

Here's one way I see you loving God with your whole heart, soul, and strength:

____

____

____

Your turn:

____

____

____

God of Our Hearts, We want to love You with all that we are. Let our devotion to You shape our devotion in our relationship. Help us spur each other on in joyful faith. May our home always be a place where love for You runs deep and overflows into every corner of our lives. Amen.

WHEN HE ARRIVED AND SAW WHAT THE GRACE OF GOD HAD DONE, HE WAS GLAD AND ENCOURAGED THEM ALL TO REMAIN TRUE TO THE LORD WITH ALL THEIR HEARTS.

—ACTS 11:23 (NIV)

What has the grace of God done in our lives? So much. It meets us with mercy, keeps no record of wrongs, and never runs out. When we forgive quickly, speak gently, and love through the mess, we reflect that same grace. What a gift—to receive such love from God and offer it freely to each other.

This is where I have seen the grace of God at work in our relationship:

____

____

____

Your turn:

____

____

____

Gracious One, Look at what Your grace has done! You've softened our hearts, strengthened our bond, and reminded us that love doesn't keep score. May we never stop rejoicing for this gift of grace and may it always lead the way in our life together. Amen.

“‘For in him we live and move and have our being.’”

—ACTS 17:28A (NIV)

We’re moving through life together—sometimes at full speed, sometimes in slow steps. Maybe it’s dancing in the kitchen, morning runs, spontaneous road trips, or just stretching out side by side after a long day. The way our bodies move and sync and adjust to each other over time is special. In our movement, there’s connection. In our energy, there’s God.

The kind of together movement that brings me the most joy:

____

____

____

Your turn:

____

____

____

God of Life and Motion, Thank You for the rhythm You've given our relationship. For the dances, the walks, the playful sprints, and even the tired shuffles. Help us to keep moving forward with joy and grace. And may we always find our being in You—and in the togetherness You've created between us. Amen.

THEREFORE ENCOURAGE ONE ANOTHER AND BUILD UP EACH OTHER, AS INDEED YOU ARE DOING.

—1 THESSALONIANS 5:11 (NRSVUE)

Sometimes, we need someone else to help us see what's already true. That's one of the beautiful parts of walking through life together. We get to remind each other of our strengths when they feel forgotten, to call out the good when it's hard to see, and to speak truth over one another with love.

Gifts I see in you that you might not always recognize in yourself:

____

____

____

Your turn:

____

____

____

Giver of Every Good Gift, Thank You for the strengths, talents, and beauty You've placed within each of us. Help us to be gentle mirrors for one another—reflecting back what is good and true when it's hard to see. May our words be full of encouragement and grace, always pointing back to You. Amen.

Rejoice with those who rejoice.

—ROMANS 12:15A (NIV)

Some celebrations are big—anniversaries, answered prayers, new beginnings. Others are small but just as sweet—an ordinary Tuesday with takeout and laughter, a shared inside joke, a tiny personal win. In this life we're building together, we want to be the kind of couple that celebrates often and well. Because joy multiplies when it's shared. And we have so much to be grateful for.

Some of our favorite ways to celebrate:

Joyful Giver, Thank You for the reasons to celebrate and the gift of someone to celebrate with. Help us notice every good thing and lift it up with joy. May our love always make room for gladness. Amen.

EVEN BEFORE A WORD IS ON MY TONGUE, O LORD, YOU KNOW IT COMPLETELY.

—PSALM 139:4 (NRSVUE)

Only the Lord knows us through and through, all at once. What we know of each other is just the beginning, but love keeps revealing more. We each carry unexpected strengths, quirks, dreams, and depths that continue to surprise and delight. Even when we think we know someone completely, there's always more to discover. That's part of the beauty of growing together.

One of the biggest (and best) surprises I've learned about you:

Your turn:

God Who Knows Us Deeply, Thank You for creating us with layers of personality, story, and soul. Help us to never stop learning about each other and loving each new discovery. May our curiosity grow alongside our commitment, drawing us ever closer in love and understanding. Amen.

The Lord will watch over your coming and going both now and forevermore.

—PSALM 121:8 (NIV)

Every trip we've taken holds a memory. The winding roads, the tucked-away cafés, the hotels with all levels of stars, even the late-night gas station snacks—we've collected them all like souvenirs in our hearts. Whether it was a long-anticipated vacation or a spontaneous weekend away, travel gave us time to connect, laugh, and learn more about each other.

Some favorite places we've traveled together:

____

____

____

Destinations still in our dreams:

____

____

____

Faithful Guide, Thank You for every mile we've traveled together. Thank You for the memories we've made and the ways we've grown along the way. Whether near or far, help us to keep seeing the world—and each other—with wonder, gratitude, and love. Amen.

DEAR CHILDREN, LET US NOT LOVE WITH WORDS OR SPEECH BUT WITH ACTIONS AND IN TRUTH.

—1 JOHN 3:18 (NIV)

We don't show up for each other just to check things off a list or keep score. And it's not for accolades or recognition or to elevate our status. We do it all out of love, following Jesus's example. The little things matter. A poured cup of coffee. A gentle touch. A chore done without asking. These are the everyday expressions of care that speak louder than words.

This simple thing makes me feel so loved by you:

____

____

____

Your turn:

____

____

____

God of Love, Thank You for the quiet ways love shows up in our relationship. Help us not to overlook the small moments, but to recognize and celebrate them as sacred acts of service and care. May our love carry the same grace and strength You show us every day. Amen.

Teach us to number our days, that we may gain a heart of wisdom.

—PSALM 90:12 (NIV)

It can be easy to slip into the rhythm of busy. But we don't want to become ships passing in the night. We want to keep showing up for one another with presence, not just productivity. The memories we make, the little traditions we build, the time we carve out to just be together—those are the treasures we'll hold close for a lifetime.

One small tradition we've created that means a lot to me:

____

____

____

Your turn:

____

____

____

Life Giver, Thank You for the gift of time and the chance to live it alongside one another. Help us to honor our days by spending them well—with laughter, intention, and devotion. Let the traditions we share together tell the story of Your love woven into ours. Amen.

YES, THE LORD HAS DONE AMAZING THINGS FOR US! WHAT JOY!

—PSALM 126:3 (NLT)

Some milestones are big—moves, promotions, new chapters. Others can go unseen—just getting through a hard day. No matter the size, every win is worth celebrating. Each one is a sign of God's faithfulness and the strength we've built together. These victories remind us just how far we've come, how far we're going, and how grateful we are to be on this journey hand in hand.

Together, let's name and celebrate some moments when we saw God move and our love grow:

____

____

____

____

____

____

____

God of Every Victory, Thank You for the milestones that have shaped our story. You help us grow stronger, wiser, and closer with each one. Teach us to pause and give thanks often—for the breakthroughs, the healing, the joy, and the love we keep building day by day. Amen.

“But as for me and my household, we will serve the Lord.”

—JOSHUA 24:15B (NRSVUE)

It’s easy to look outward and feel pressure to be doing all the things to make a difference in the world. But one of the most powerful ways we reflect God’s love is in how we care for each other at home. Our family is a sacred calling—our first ministry, our closest community. Every act of love, every shared prayer, and every moment of laughter or forgiveness matters.

One way I see us making our household holy ground:

____

____

____

Your turn:

____

____

____

♥

Lord of Our Home, Thank You for the gift of this family and the calling to love one another well. Help us to serve each other with joy and grace, and to see our home as a place of purpose and presence. Show us when to say no so we can say yes to what matters most. Amen.

SO LET'S NOT GET TIRED OF DOING WHAT IS GOOD. AT JUST THE RIGHT TIME WE WILL REAP A HARVEST OF BLESSING IF WE DON'T GIVE UP.

—GALATIANS 6:9 (NLT)

Some days, love feels like work. Stress, hardship, or weariness can chip away at joy. But through every challenge, we've stood together. This love is worth protecting, worth tending, worth fighting for. Not out of obligation, but because this love is a gift. A beautiful, God-given thing that we are building together, day by day.

A time you fought for us—and I really felt it—was . . .

____

____

____

Your turn:

____

____

____

Our Good God, Thank You for this love that's worth fighting for. When we face trials, remind us that You're in the center—strengthening our resolve, softening our hearts, and helping us rise again. Help us to protect what we've been given and to keep showing up with courage, tenderness, and grace. Amen.

“The joy of the Lord is your strength.”

—NEHEMIAH 8:10B (NRSVUE)

Joy doesn’t always mean big smiles or perfect days. Sometimes joy looks like a quiet moment with a favorite book, a long walk with a friend, or a meal shared after a hard week. God delights in our delight—and we believe He designed us to experience joy both on our own and side by side. Joy is a gift.

Here's what makes our hearts light up:

Giver of Joy, Thank You for weaving gladness into our days. Help us to recognize and protect the things that bring us joy—individually and together. May our home be filled with laughter, gratitude, and moments that reflect the delight You take in us. Amen.

THEN MY PEOPLE WILL LIVE IN A PLACE OF PEACE, IN SAFE HOMES, AND IN QUIET RESTING PLACES.

—ISAIAH 32:18 (NLV)

Our home is more than a place—it's the backdrop of our love story. It holds our laughter, our dreams, and the comfort we've built through God's grace. But more than anything, home is you and me together. Wherever we go, whatever we face, as long as we're side by side, we're home. And there's no place like it.

This is what I think makes our home feel most like "us":

____

____

____

Your turn:

____

____

____

Heavenly Father, Thank You for the shelter of our home and the sanctuary of our love. How beautiful are the warmth, safety, and joy we feel when we're together—wherever that may be! May our home always be a place of peace, a reflection of Your goodness, and a haven where love lives and grows. Amen.

"You are the light of the world. A town built on a hill cannot be hidden."

—MATTHEW 5:14 (NIV)

Light and love—this is what we want to be. Some of the most sacred moments in our relationship are when I see you light up—fully alive, fully yourself, fully shining. Christ's light is in you, and it shines through you. Let's keep watching for those moments in each other. Let's name them, celebrate them, and carry that light into every space we share.

This is one time I've seen you shine with the light and love of Christ:

Your turn:

Light of the World, Thank You for placing Your light within us—and between us. Help us to notice and nurture the moments when each of us shines. Let our love reflect Your love. Let our home reflect Your light. And may the joy we find in each other spill out into every place we go. Amen.

CARRY EACH OTHER'S BURDENS, AND IN THIS WAY YOU WILL FULFILL THE LAW OF CHRIST.

—GALATIANS 6:2 (NIV)

Not every fix needs a wrench. Some of the most meaningful repairs in our relationship didn't involve tools at all. Just a hug after an argument, a shared laugh that breaks the tension, or the courage to say "I'm sorry." In big ways and small, we're learning how to mend what's been cracked. And every repair has only made us stronger.

One "repair" during a difficult moment or season that meant so much to me:

____

____

____

Your turn:

____

____

____

Great Healing God, Thank You for the strength to mend what's broken—inside and out. Remind us that even small acts of care can heal deep places. Help us offer patience, forgiveness, and a sense of humor when things go sideways. Thank You for making us a team—not perfect, but always growing stronger together. Amen.

For we are God's coworkers, working together.

—1 CORINTHIANS 3:9A (NRSVUE)

We've each been given unique gifts, but something powerful happens when we use them together. Our relationship isn't just about love—it's about calling. Whether we're raising a family, serving others, or simply showing up with kindness, we've been placed here side by side on purpose, for a purpose. We get to build something meaningful that shows God's love in action.

One way I've seen God using our relationship for something bigger than ourselves:

____

____

____

Your turn:

____

____

____

Purposeful God, Thank You for bringing us together—not just to love each other, but to love the world better together. Help us keep our eyes open to the places You are calling us to serve, lead, grow, and give. May we always say yes to what matters most. Amen.

FOR SINCE THE WORLD BEGAN, NO EAR HAS HEARD AND NO EYE HAS SEEN A GOD LIKE YOU, WHO WORKS FOR THOSE WHO WAIT FOR HIM!

—ISAIAH 64:4 (NLT)

We once dreamed of being here—together. And now, by God's grace, that dream is reality. What a gift to build a life with someone who believes in you, dreams with you, and cheers you on. Let's keep encouraging each other to dream boldly, step bravely, and trust that God is already working behind the scenes.

One dream I'm holding in my heart:

___

___

___

Your turn:

___

___

___

Dream Giver, Thank You for planting dreams in our hearts—dreams both for ourselves and for our future together. Make a way for these dreams to come true. We believe and trust that they will—all in Your perfect time—as You guide every step. Amen.

"Be strong and courageous. Do not be afraid; do not be discouraged, for the LORD your God will be with you wherever you go."

—JOSHUA 1:9B (NIV)

Some fears are healthy—like avoiding tornadoes or sleeping bears. But others hold us back: fear of failure, rejection, not being enough. What if we faced those fears together? What if we encouraged each other to step out in faith—toward the dreams, callings, and adventures God has placed on our hearts? Together, we can choose courage over comfort and trust His leading.

A leap of faith that brought us closer to each other and to God:

____

____

____

Your turn:

____

____

____

Fear Breaker, Help us to lean into faith—and each other—to take brave steps. We don't want to miss the gifts that lie waiting on the other side of the barrier of fear. Remind us that love, when rooted in You, casts out fear. Help us to chase the dreams You've placed in our hearts with boldness and joy. Amen.

AND NOW THESE THREE REMAIN: FAITH, HOPE AND LOVE. BUT THE GREATEST OF THESE IS LOVE.

—1 CORINTHIANS 13:13 (NIV)

Our love is a powerful force. But it's not always grand gestures or dramatic declarations. More often, it's a hand to hold, a shared glance, simple understanding. Our love is felt daily in comfort, joy, and presence. A shoulder to cry on, a smile of encouragement, the choice to show up for each other again and again. We may not always see it, but we live it. And that's everything.

This is what our love feels like in everyday moments:

Your turn:

God of Love, Thank You for the beautiful (though often private) strength of our relationship that carries us through the good times and the bad. Lead us to express our love freely, feel it deeply, and honor it always. May we never take such a gift for granted. Amen.

Your ears will hear a word behind you, saying, "This is the way, walk in it," whenever you turn to the right or to the left.

—ISAIAH 30:21 (NLV)

A conversation. A hard decision. A "yes" that led to something more. We don't always see the turn coming, but when we look back, we realize—we were never the same after that. God often works through these turning points to draw us closer to Him, and to each other. They remind us that love isn't stagnant—it's always growing and stretching.

A turning point in our story that stands out to me:

____

____

____

Your turn:

____

____

____

♥

Light on Our Path, Thank You for the moments that change everything. For the hard-won clarity, the new directions, and the grace You give to help us grow through it all. Keep our hearts open to what You're doing next, and help us walk every new path hand in hand. Amen.

I AM MY BELOVED'S, AND MY BELOVED IS MINE.

—SONG OF SONGS 6:3A (NRSVUE)

Sometimes it feels like you know me better than I know myself. You notice what I haven't said, sense my mood before I do, and speak what I most need to hear. That kind of knowing is a sacred bond that reflects the way God knits two hearts together in love. I hope I meet your needs too, in the ways that matter most.

When you do [*this*], you really meet [*this need*]:

____

____

____

Your turn:

____

____

____

Maker of Heaven and Earth, Thank You for bringing our souls together and creating this deep love. Open our eyes and hearts to each other's needs and guide us to respond with grace, presence, and love. May we continue to grow in understanding and compassion. Amen.

A cord of three strands is not quickly broken.

—ECCLESIASTES 4:12B (NIV)

Life can pull us in countless directions, sometimes leaving us feeling like we're barely keeping our heads above water. In those moments, we cling tightly to God and each other—our strong cord of three strands. A hand held through exhaustion, an embrace after a long day, a shoulder to lean on when words fail: Our physical closeness becomes a reminder that we're not alone.

**This is how I love you to hold on to me—
physically, emotionally, or spiritually—
when life feels overwhelming:**

____

____

____

Your turn:

____

____

____

Our Steady Strength, We know that You see us, hear us, love us, feel with us. In the busy seasons, the heavy seasons, the barely-holding-it-together seasons, help us to come near to You and to wrap our arms around each other. We are so grateful we can confidently say that we are in this—all of it—together, with You. Amen.

PLANS FAIL FOR LACK OF COUNSEL, BUT WITH MANY ADVISERS THEY SUCCEED.

—PROVERBS 15:22 (NIV)

We weren't meant to walk this journey alone. Throughout our relationship, God has placed people in our lives who have guided, encouraged, and spoken wisdom into us. Their steady voices and faithful lives have helped shape our own. These wise mentors—whether parents, pastors, or friends—remind us that God often works through others to strengthen our love and our faith.

I appreciate this wisdom that has been given to us in love from a special person:

____

____

____

Your turn:

____

____

____

Wise One, Thank You for the people You've placed in our lives to walk with us, challenge us, and pour wisdom into our hearts. Help us to listen well, honor those who have come before us, and carry their guidance forward with grace and gratitude. May we also grow into people who speak wisdom into others. Amen.

Let the redeemed of the Lord tell their story.

—PSALM 107:2A (NIV)

The stories in movies have a way of bringing us closer—whether we're curled up with popcorn watching an old favorite, quoting lines from that one film we've seen a hundred times, or discovering a new film that sparks conversation or emotion. They make us laugh, cry, reflect, and dream.

What are a few of our movie memories—funny, romantic, or meaningful?

If our love story were a movie, what would the title be?

God of Joy and Imagination, Thank You for stories that move us and memories that bring us closer. Help us continue to share moments filled with laughter, wonder, and love—both on screen and in real life. Amen.

HE SAYS, "BE STILL, AND KNOW THAT I AM GOD."

—PSALM 46:10A (NIV)

Stillness doesn't come easily in the rhythms of everyday life. There are always tasks pressing in and tugging at our time. But when we choose stillness, even in small moments, the reward is great. We begin to notice what matters most, hear God clearly, and rediscover each other.

Some ways we appreciate stillness in our life together:

Great I AM, In You we find calm when our world spins fast. Help us to slow down, breathe deeply, and be still with You and with each other. In those quiet yet connected moments, may we abide in peace and grow in trust and love. Amen.

Even though I walk through the valley of the shadow of death, I will fear no evil, for you are with me. Your rod and your staff, they comfort me.

—PSALM 23:4 (WEB)

The thought of us not being together is a hard one to bear, but the truth is, our lives here on earth are temporary. They are like the blink of an eye. Thankfully, we have peace knowing that we will be together for all of eternity, with our Father above. Our thoughts rest on our Shepherd, His comfort, and His promise that this isn't the end of our story.

When I think of our eternity with God, here's what I picture . . .

Your turn:

Tender Shepherd, Thank You for walking beside us in every valley. Your love holds us when our hearts are breaking into teeny-tiny pieces all around. Give us a glimpse of Your eternal comfort in ways we can feel now. Help us carry each other gently through grief, always anchored in Your heavenly hope. Amen.

SO THEN,
JUST AS YOU
RECEIVED CHRIST
JESUS AS LORD,
CONTINUE TO LIVE
YOUR LIVES IN HIM,
ROOTED AND BUILT UP
IN HIM, STRENGTHENED
IN THE FAITH AS YOU
WERE TAUGHT, AND
OVERFLOWING WITH
THANKFULNESS.

—COLOSSIANS 2:6–7 (NIV)

Love doesn't stand still. It grows. Over time, we change, individually and together. The way we love today looks different than when we started—and that's a beautiful thing. Our roots are deeper. Our faith is stronger. Our bond is richer.

These are the ways in which we've grown that I'm the most thankful for:

____

____

____

Your turn:

____

____

____

God Who Grows Us, Thank You for the journey You've taken us on. Through every change, You've shaped us, stretched us, and drawn us closer—to You and to each other. Keep growing our love, Lord. Let it be strong, steady, and full of grace. Amen.

Let love and faithfulness never leave you; bind them around your neck, write them on the tablet of your heart.

—PROVERBS 3:3 (NIV)

One day, when the stories of our life together are told, what do we hope people remember? Maybe it's the way we laughed often, forgave quickly, and never let go of one another—no matter what came our way. Maybe it's how we made others feel welcome, safe, and seen. How will God use our legacy of love to share His love?

What I hope people will say about our love story:

____

____

____

Your turn:

____

____

____

Everlasting God, Thank You for this love that shapes our days and leaves a mark beyond ourselves. Help us live in a way that reflects Your goodness. May the way we love one another become a light that points to You and blesses those who come after. Amen.

FOR THIS GOD IS OUR GOD FOR EVER AND EVER; HE WILL BE OUR GUIDE EVEN TO THE END.

—PSALM 48:14 (NIV)

As we come to the final pages of this journal, our hearts are full. We've shared memories, prayers, and hopes. This may be the end of these written words, but it's not the end of our story. Wherever the path leads, we'll walk it together—anchored in love and led by God. Always. Forever. Faithfully.

A hope I carry for our future, trusting God to make a way:

____

____

____

Your turn:

____

____

____

Our God Forever and Ever, We praise You for this sacred time we have cherished with one another and with You. As we step into the chapters still ahead, may we move forward with peace and confidence, knowing You are leading us—every step, every season. Let our love continue to deepen as we lean not on our own understanding, but always on You. Amen.